LANGUAGE ARTS

EXPLORER JUNIOR

How to Write a Comic Book

by Nel Yomtov

Published in the United States of America by Cherry Lake Publishing
Ann Arbor, Michigan
www.cherrylakepublishing.com

Content Adviser: Gail Dickinson, PhD, Associate Professor, Old Dominion
University, Norfolk, Virginia

Photo Credits: Page 10, ©Picture Partners/Alamy; page 16, ©matka_
Wariatka/Shutterstock, Inc.

Library of Congress Cataloging-in-Publication Data
Yomtov, Nelson.
  How to write a comic book / by Nel Yomtov.
      pages cm. – (Language Arts Explorer Junior)
  Includes bibliographical references and index.
  ISBN 978-1-62431-187-1 (lib. bdg.) – ISBN 978-1-62431-253-3
(e-book) – ISBN 978-1-62431-319-6 (pbk.)
  1. Comic books, strips, etc.–Authorship–Juvenile literature. 2. Graphic
novels–Authorship–Juvenile literature. I. Title.

  PN6710.Y66 2013
  741.5'1–dc23   2013006657

Cherry Lake Publishing would like to acknowledge the work
of The Partnership for 21st Century Skills. Please visit www.p21.org
for more information.

Printed in the United States of America
Corporate Graphics, Inc.
July 2013
CLFA13

Table of Contents

CHAPTER ONE

Be a Super Storyteller! 4

CHAPTER TWO

Tips from the Pros 6

CHAPTER THREE

Creating Characters 9

CHAPTER FOUR

Telling Your Story 13

CHAPTER FIVE

Putting It All Together 16

Glossary 22

For More Information 23

Index 24

About the Author 24

Be a Super Storyteller!

When was the last time you read a comic book? Comic books are a great way of telling interesting stories. They can contain a lot of words or be totally wordless. They can be funny or sad. Some are printed in color. Others are in black and white. Comics can tell **fictional** stories. They can also detail real-life events.

All comic books use pictures. The pictures are arranged in an order that tells a story or expresses thoughts and feelings.

Writing a comic book allows you to make up interesting characters and places. It also lets you tell weird and wonderful stories. The sky is the limit when you are a comic book writer!

Lettering is any text on a comic book page. Most comic book lettering is uppercase.

Bold lettering is used to emphasize important words. Large lettering is used to indicate shouting. Small lettering is used to indicate whispering.

A WORD BALLOON CONTAINS THE DIALOGUE THAT A CHARACTER SPEAKS.

A THOUGHT BALLOON CONTAINS THOUGHTS A CHARACTER DOES NOT SPEAK.

A word balloon contains the dialogue that a character speaks. It has a "tail" that points to the speaker. Word balloons come in all shapes and sizes.

A thought balloon contains thoughts a character does not speak. The tail looks like a trail of bubbles.

Panel: a single image in a sequence of images

Border: a line that encloses panels, balloons, and captions

Gutter: the space between and around panels

POW!

Sound effects represent noises in a scene. Most sound effects are floating letters.

A CAPTION IS USED FOR NARRATION, OR WORDS THAT ARE USED TO HELP TELL THE STORY. CAPTIONS USUALLY HAVE RECTANGULAR BORDERS.

CHAPTER TWO

Tips from the Pros

You can write a comic book about anything you can imagine. Here are a few writing tips before you begin:

- Learn from the pros. Pay careful attention when you're watching a movie or a TV show. Is the dialogue realistic? Did the **plot** make sense?

- Create interesting, original characters. Your characters must be colorful and unique in some way. Your readers must care about both the good guys and the bad guys.
- Write about things that interest you. The more interest you have in your subject, the easier it will be to make your comic book interesting for your readers.
- Write about things you know. If you don't know enough about your subject, learn more about it online or in the library.
- Don't stop writing. Writing becomes easier the more you do it. Try to develop a regular writing schedule.
- Keep at it! Don't get discouraged if you think your first few comic book stories aren't very good. You will get better with practice!

ACTIVITY

Getting Started

Come up with some ideas for a story. Make a list of the things you already know. Then make a list of the things you want to learn about.

INSTRUCTIONS:
1. Draw a line down the middle of a piece of notebook paper.
2. Write "Subjects I Know" at the top of the left side. Write "Subjects I Like" at the top of the right side.
3. Under "Subjects I Know," make a list of the things you know a lot about.
4. Under "Subjects I Like," make a list of the things you're interested in but don't know a lot about. You'll need to research these subjects if you want to write a story about them.

To get a copy of this activity, visit www.cherrylakepublishing.com/activities.

CHAPTER THREE

Creating Characters

You've decided what you want to write about. Now it's time to think about who you're writing about. Your **script** describes each panel and page of your comic. It contains all of your dialogue and captions. But you have to create interesting characters before you begin writing your script.

Your characters must be believable. They should have emotions and goals just like real people do. They should face problems like real people do. The relationships they have with other characters should be interesting. These relationships reveal information about the characters' backgrounds and personalities.

Every person in real life is different. Each of your characters should also be different.

What are the characters like in your favorite comics?

Maybe one character has a good sense of humor. Another never cracks a smile. Perhaps one character suffers from an illness. Another might have a special talent.

Give each character a **conflict**. Conflict is the main ingredient of an interesting story. Each character has goals. Conflict is something that stands in the way of these goals. Realistic conflict will help make the characters believable to your readers.

Make a Chart

You've thought about your characters. Now you need to organize your thoughts. A chart can help you do this. Look at the chart on page 12. It shows one way to describe a character in a comic book story. Make a similar chart for each of your comic book characters.

HERE'S WHAT YOU'LL NEED:
- Notebook paper
- Ruler
- Pencil

INSTRUCTIONS:
1. Use a ruler to help you draw four boxes on a piece of paper.
2. Label your chart in the same way as the boxes on page 12.
3. Fill in the boxes of your chart with information about your character.

To get a copy of this activity, visit www.cherrylakepublishing.com/activities.

TITLE OF STORY: Mission to Mars!

AUTHOR: Randi Morris

NAME OF CHARACTER: Lieutenant James Briggs

BACKGROUND INFORMATION:
- Born in Dallas, Texas
- 37 years old; married; two children
- 5 feet 10 inches tall; 210 pounds
- Served in U.S. Air Force
- Astronaut for six years
- Journey to Mars is his first space voyage

PERSONALITY:
- Always wants to win and be in charge
- Gets angry easily
- Expects hard work from his crew

WHAT HE WANTS:
- For the mission to Mars to be successful
- To become famous
- To prove to his co-commander on the mission that he's the number one leader

WHAT'S IN HIS WAY (Conflict):
- Crew blames him for problems with the spacecraft while in flight
- Co-commander beginning to take control of the mission

CHAPTER FOUR

Telling Your Story

The stories in most comic books are divided into a beginning, middle, and end. This type of storytelling is called a three-act structure. The beginning is called the first act. It introduces the main characters and the main conflict. It also describes the **setting**. The middle is called the second act. It adds further challenges for the characters. This increases the feeling of suspense in the story. The third act is the end. It presents the main solution to the conflict. It shows how characters and situations have changed throughout the story. This is the thrilling conclusion of the story.

I WONDER HOW THIS IS GOING TO END.

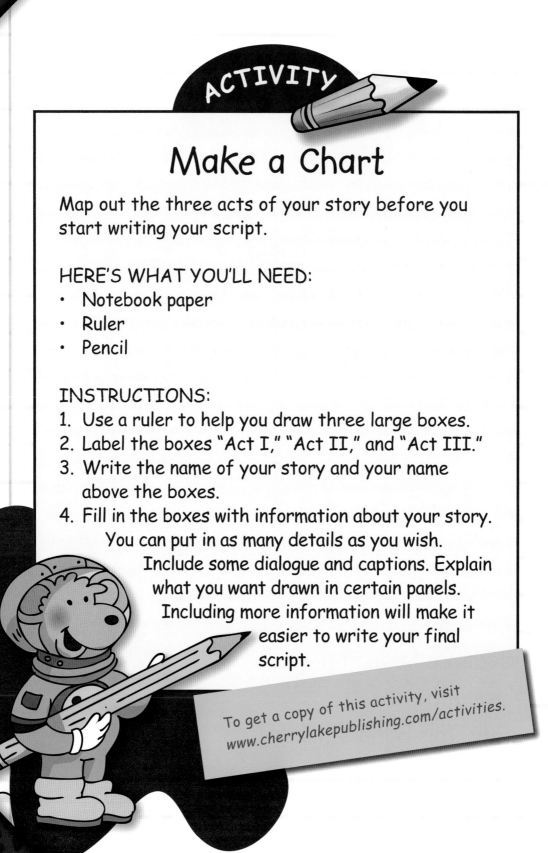

Make a Chart

Map out the three acts of your story before you start writing your script.

HERE'S WHAT YOU'LL NEED:
- Notebook paper
- Ruler
- Pencil

INSTRUCTIONS:
1. Use a ruler to help you draw three large boxes.
2. Label the boxes "Act I," "Act II," and "Act III."
3. Write the name of your story and your name above the boxes.
4. Fill in the boxes with information about your story. You can put in as many details as you wish. Include some dialogue and captions. Explain what you want drawn in certain panels. Including more information will make it easier to write your final script.

To get a copy of this activity, visit www.cherrylakepublishing.com/activities.

TITLE: Mission to Mars!

WRITER: Randi Morris

THREE-ACT STRUCTURE:
ACT I

- We meet Briggs and his crew members as they blast off from the launchpad.
- We learn about Briggs's strong personality.
- We get a sense of some of the crew's doubts about Briggs's leadership abilities.
- Act I ends with a dramatic scene: some of the onboard computers malfunction.

ACT II

- We cover Briggs's response to the malfunctioning. Things still aren't totally fixed, and the crew begins to disobey him.
- More trouble arises: The spacecraft gets caught in an asteroid field. It is struck by many small asteroids.
- Briggs safely gets the craft out of the asteroid field.

ACT III

- Briggs directs the repairs of the onboard computers. The crew follows his commands.
- The spacecraft drops to the surface of Mars. Briggs's quick thinking has made the journey a success!

Putting It All Together

Have fun and be creative as you think of details for your script.

You've worked out the rough plot of your story. You've created your characters. Now it's time to put it all together and start writing.

Start by describing the settings where the action takes place. Be as specific as you can. Is it a large city? A laboratory? The inside of a spacecraft? Is it nighttime? Is it raining? Adding details to your story will hook your readers and keep them interested.

Finding clever ways to move from scene to scene while continuing the mood of your story is also important. Some writers use dialogue or captions to do this. A character named John might say, "I will never eat a bologna sandwich again!" The next panel shows John's sister making a bologna sandwich for him. She is thinking, "John is going to be so excited when he sees that I made lunch!" Don't hesitate to move back and forth between scenes. Many superhero writers break up long fight scenes by moving to ones where characters are just talking.

Mission to Mars!

by Randi Morris

Artists: David Day and Anita Perez

PAGE 1

PANEL 1

ART DIRECTIONS: One big panel, called a splash page, showing a large rocket blasting off from a launchpad. Lots of fire and smoke pouring out from the huge engines. Bright, sunny day.

CAPTION: Today, mankind takes its **boldest** step in humanity's quest of the stars.

CAPTION: Aboard the giant spacecraft are five of the most highly trained astronauts ever sent into space.

SOUND EFFECTS (SFX): VROOOOSH!

PAGE 2

PANEL 1

ART DIRECTIONS: Medium shot. Inside the spacecraft. Show all five astronauts in their seats. They are wearing their space suits and helmets. (Artists, please use the reference I provided when I gave you the script.) Each astronaut is looking at a computer screen while working some controls.

BRIGGS DIALOGUE: **Anderson**, how is liftoff looking?

ANDERSON DIALOGUE: All systems A-OK, **Lieutenant Briggs**.

BRIGGS THOUGHT BALLOON: Let's just hope it's a smooth ride to Mars.

PANEL 2

ART DIRECTIONS: Close-up on Briggs as he speaks to his crew.

BRIGGS DIALOGUE: We trained **months** for this mission. Let's show the world what we can do!

BRIGGS DIALOGUE: We should be hearing from mission control any minute.

PANEL 3

ART DIRECTIONS: Long shot that shows the mission control building back on Earth.

BALLOON POINTER TO BUILDING: Mission control to Alpha I. Do you read us?

PANEL 4

ART DIRECTIONS: Medium shot inside mission control. Several men and women crowd around a TV monitor. They are well dressed. The men wear pants and white shirts with ties. The women are dressed in business suits. On the TV monitor we see the astronauts inside the spacecraft. One of the technicians speaks to Briggs.

BRIGGS DIALOGUE; BALLOON POINTER TO TV MONITOR: We read you, mission control. All systems look good.

TECHNICIAN DIALOGUE: Everything going exactly as planned. Liftoff was **perfect**.

TECHNICIAN DIALOGUE: Get some rest—it's going to be a **long** flight!

LET'S SHOW THE WORLD WHAT WE CAN DO!

Every comic book script must contain art directions for the artist who's going to draw the story. Describe what should be in each panel. This includes the setting and what the characters are doing. Art directions also describe how characters are dressed, their emotions, and any other details you can think of. Should the panel be a close-up? Close-ups are a great way to show emotion or strong drama. Should the panel be a medium shot? Medium shots are good for showing where characters are positioned in the setting. A long shot is good for introducing a new setting. Mix up your selection of shots as you write your script to vary the mood of your story.

Good luck—and happy comic book writing!

Finishing Your Comic Book Script

Now it's time to put your finished script together. Take a look at the sample on the previous spread before you begin.

INSTRUCTIONS:
1. Write the name of your story, your name, and the artist's name at the top of the first page of your script.
2. For each panel, provide art directions for the artist.
3. Write the dialogue, captions, and sound effects that you wish to appear in each panel.
4. Make sure your script—no matter how long or short it is—has a beginning, middle, and end. Your story should have a lot of drama and conflict to keep your readers interested.
5. Read your script after you've finished writing. This will help you find mistakes or places where you can improve your story.

To get a copy of this activity, visit www.cherrylakepublishing.com/activities.

VROOOOSH!

Glossary

conflict (KAHN-flikt) struggle or disagreement

dialogue (DYE-uh-lawg) conversation, especially in a play, movie, TV show, or book

fictional (FIK-shuh-nuhl) made up

narration (na-RAY-shuhn) words describing the things that are happening in a story

plot (PLAHT) the main story of a comic book or any other work of fiction

script (SKRIPT) a panel-by-panel, page-by-page document that describes all the details of a comic book story

setting (SET-ing) the time period and location where a story takes place

For More Information

BOOKS

Roche, Art. *Comic Strips: Create Your Own Comic Strips from Start to Finish*; New York: Sterling, 2011.

Rosinsky, Natalie M. *Graphic Novel*. Minneapolis: Compass Point Books, 2009.

WEB SITES

Creative Comic Art—Writing a Comic Script
www.creativecomicart.com/writing-comics.html
Learn the basics of good visual storytelling.

HowStuffWorks—How Comic Books Work
http://entertainment.howstuffworks.com/arts/comic-books/comic-book.htm
Read how comic books have made a huge impact on American culture.

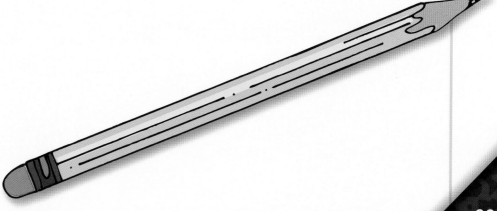

Index

art directions, 18, 19, 20, 21

borders, 5

captions, 5, 9, 14, 17, 18, 21
characters, 4, 5, 7, 9–10, 11, 12, 13, 17, 20
charts, 11–12, 14
close-ups, 20
colors, 4
conclusions, 13, 15
conflict, 10, 12, 13, 17, 21

details, 14, 17, 20
dialogue, 5, 6, 9, 14, 17, 18, 19, 21

first act, 13, 15

gutters, 5

ideas, 8

lettering, 5
long shots, 20

medium shots, 20
mood, 17, 20
movies, 6

narration, 5

panels, 5, 9, 14, 20, 21
personalities, 9, 10, 12
plots, 6
practice, 7

scripts, 9, 14, 18–19, 20, 21
second act, 13, 15
settings, 4, 13, 17, 20
sound effects, 5, 18, 21
subjects, 7, 8

television shows, 6
third act, 13, 15
thought balloons, 5
three-act structure, 13, 14, 15

word balloons, 5

About the Author

Nel Yomtov is an award-winning author of nonfiction books and graphic novels for young readers. He has worked at Marvel Comics as a writer, editor, and colorist. He also served as Marvel's director of product development, supervising the creation of products that used the Marvel Comics characters, including toys, clothing, books, and calendars.